Medieval People

Sarah Howarth

MACDONALD YOUNG BOOKS

For Philip

First published in Great Britain in 1991 by

Simon & Schuster Young Books

Reprinted 1994 by
Macdonald Young Books
Campus 400
Maylands Avenue
Hemel Hempstead
Herts HP2 7EZ

Text copyright © 1991 by Sarah Howarth
Illustrations copyright © 1991 by Philip McNeill

Typeset by DP Press Ltd, Sevenoaks

Printed and bound by Proost International Book Co., Belgium

British Library Cataloguing in Publication Data

Howarth, Sarah
  Medieval people.
  I. Title
  941.02

  ISBN 0750008792

Picture Acknowledgements

Picture research by Jennie Karrach

Front cover: Bibliotheque Nationale, Paris
Spine: Giraudon

All interior pictures reproduced by courtesy of the Trustees
of the British Library except:
Archiv Für Kunst und Geschichte: p.13
Bibliotheque Nationale, Paris: p.8, p.44
Biblioteca Nazionale Marziana, Venice: p.26
Cumbria County Archive: p.29
Reproduced by permission of the Provost and Fellows of
  Eton College: p.34
E.T. Archive: p.37
Sonia Halliday Photos: p.22, p.23, p.31, p.38, p.43
Robert Harding Picture Library: p.41
Michael Holford Photographs: p.10, p.12, p.14, p.20, p.21,
  p.24, p.27, p.39
By permission of the Masters and Fellows of Trinity College,
  Cambridge: p.36

CONTENTS

INTRODUCTION

Imagine you had to tell someone from another planet about the world we live in today. How would you do it? One way would be to describe different sorts of people,

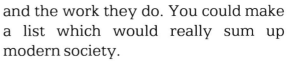

and the work they do. You could make a list which would really sum up modern society.

This book will introduce you to some medieval people and the world in which they lived. Like your imaginary list, the selection of people itself will give you a lot of information about the Middle Ages. Many of the people on the list are men, because women had little position in medieval society, and a limited range of opportunities. The most important men were noblemen and men of the Church, who had a great deal of wealth and power. Many of the people described in the book were prosperous, because the poor did not attract the attention of medieval writers, and so we know less about them.

The book will tell you about the work and the way of life of different medieval people. It will also explain something of their religious beliefs, pastimes, family life, trade, buildings, politics and medicine. These things will help you understand what it was like to live in the Middle Ages.

THE CHRONICLER

This is the voice of an Irish monk and writer who lived in the ninth century:

'Myself and White Pangur the cat are each at his own trade. He has his mind on hunting, my mind is on my own task. Better than any fame I prefer peace with my book.'

News bulletins from the Middle Ages

How is it that we know what happened in the Middle Ages? The people we are going to look at in this book lived anything up to 1000 years ago. How can we tell what life was like for them?

In the Middle Ages, books were luxury items. They were written by hand and decorated with illuminated pictures like this, using gold leaf and other costly materials. Only wealthy people could afford them. Here a French writer presents his book to King Charles VI.

mer. Si il aduint que enuiron
.vin. iours apzez il armia deuat
vne cite la quelle estoit bien p
fout cest a dire bien auãt situee
en mer. z pour aler a celle cite

This is a page from a medieval chronicle. Chronicles were records of events written by people who lived at the time.

The answer is that some people at the time wrote things down. They made a record of important events, and also included all sorts of other things which interested them. It was as if they were writing a kind of diary. These stories of events are called 'chronicles'.

Chroniclers were writing the news of their day. They recorded such things as the coronation of kings and queens; when countries went to war; when important men died; a great fire in a city; a bad harvest; the death of many animals in a plague, and any other news which attracted their attention.

Let's look at an English chronicle, called the *Anglo-Saxon Chronicle*, and see what it has to say. The chronicler is talking about the year 1117, but the events he notes down are typical. You would find stories like these in any chronicle, in any year in the Middle Ages.

'In this year there were violent storms, and one night the heaven seemed very red, as if there was a great fire in the sky. In January there was a great earthquake in Italy. And it was a very bad year for crops because of the rain.'

Chroniclers set down local gossip as well as events which affected the whole country. All types of information got mixed together, like births and weddings in the families of the local nobility, quarrels between great landowners, stories about local men, or new buildings in the area.

The authors of the chronicles

Many chronicles were written by monks. Few people had the leisure or the learning to write a chronicle. To do so required a peaceful, orderly environment — and access to books and information. The monastery was usually the place where these were to be found. Monks were among the few people who could read and write. Because the monastic orders to which they belonged spread over the whole of Europe, they also received news from a wide area.

The closer you look at the contents of a chronicle, the more clues you will find about the chronicler and the way he or she wrote: where they lived, what their interests were, how long it took to compose the chronicle, and so on.

Looking into the mind of the chronicler

Medieval people generally believed that God directly ruled the world and everything that happened in it. When chroniclers came to write their version of history, they were not just noting down events. They wanted to record *why* they had happened. Because of their religious beliefs, very often the explanations given were spiritual ones.

Men of the Church were among the few people who could read and write in the Middle Ages. Here you can see a bishop writing.

This is what the *Anglo-Saxon Chronicle* had to say when an English king was killed in 1100. The passage shows how the chronicler's religious beliefs affected the way he wrote: '*He was very harsh and fierce. While he was king, much evil was done. Therefore he was hated by almost all his people and by God.*'

Chroniclers give us their view of events. Their ideas coloured the way they wrote and the events they chose to write about. Historians call this bias. Like the chronicle, everything we write about history is biased in some way.

THE KING

This was one chronicler's verdict on King Edward I of England who died in 1307:

'Throughout his time he had been fearless and warlike.'

This was praise indeed.

The king and his noblemen: a struggle for power

In most countries, the nobility had all the political power. The king was the most important nobleman of all. But his position was not always secure. His power and authority depended on controlling the nobility. The chronicler's verdict on King Edward reveals one very important way in which the king could do this: by leading them into battle and waging successful wars.

Another way in which the king tried to maintain his position was by making rich gifts to the noblemen. Land was the most valuable gift that could be given. In some countries, like England and Sicily, much of the land in the kingdom was at the king's disposal. He could grant great estates to his followers, making them wealthy and important men. These estates were called fiefs.

This picture shows King Alfonso, the Wise of Castile (part of modern Spain). On the right a clerk sits writing, and a group of men stand with a book. The king needed educated men to help him govern. They were usually men of the Church.

Here you can see a Portuguese king dining with bishops and noblemen. Important political decisions were made at banquets and formal occasions like these.

In gratitude his followers made promises in return. They pledged their loyalty, swearing that first and foremost they would be the king's men. Whenever he needed advice or armed support, they would give it. The way contemporaries, people at the time, described this was to say that the king was their lord, and the followers his barons or 'vassals'.

With the estates the king gave them, the vassals could attract supporters of their own. Just like the king, they granted some of their land away in return for military support. They too acted as lords, and had their own vassals.

The king's power

Some kings had a great staff of officials all over the kingdom to see that their commands were carried out. These men were employed to collect the king's revenues and bring him information. William I of England ruled in this way.

William came from Normandy, part of modern France. In Normandy he was a powerful nobleman; when he came to England, he defeated the English army at the Battle of Hastings in 1066 and became king. This is why he was called William the Conqueror. William's officials were so efficient that they compiled a survey of

the whole country, which showed every important landholder. '*Not one cow, nor one pig escaped his attention*,' remarked one chronicler in amazement. Contemporaries, who were generally very religious, were so alarmed at this display of royal power that they felt as if God's great day of judgement had come. They nicknamed William's survey the *Domesday Book*, and that name has stuck ever since.

William had enormous power. He was in a good position to secure the obedience of his vassals. His Norman followers were eager to maintain his power because, like him, they were newcomers to the country. If he lost everything, then so would they.

The coronation of King Edward I of England in 1274. At his coronation the king vowed to rule justly.

The king's power challenged

A few generations later, the story was different. The king's vassals felt established on their land. Son succeeded father. They forgot that they once owed everything to the king. Some barons grew wealthy and powerful enough almost to rival the king. Weak or unpopular rulers found themselves challenged by such men. King John of England found himself in this position. His barons rebelled and forced him to grant them a number of privileges. These were written down in a great charter in 1215. The Latin for 'great charter' is *Magna Carta*. This is what the charter was called by the men of the time. We still call it by this name today.

These were among the promises John had to make:

'*No freeman shall be arrested except by the law of the land. We shall refuse justice to no one.*'

The promises John made in *Magna Carta* show how he had great problems with his barons. They felt that he had not treated them justly, and accused him of acting outside the law.

The events of John's reign were very dramatic. Not every king had to face armed rebellion. But all over Europe, great noblemen grew more confident and demanded a share in governing the country.

THE POPE

O ne of the most famous popes of the Middle Ages, named Innocent III, wrote in a letter: ✔

'Others may have a share of responsibility, but we alone have been given complete and absolute authority by God.'

The head of the Church

In the Middle Ages Christianity was the religion of western Europe. There was only one Church, the Catholic Church. In eastern Europe Christians belonged to the Greek Church. The pope was the Bishop of Rome and the head of the Catholic Church. Catholics believed he was the successor of St Peter the Apostle, and the leader of all Christians. The Christian Church in eastern Europe did not acknowledge these claims of the pope.

The Pope was sometimes criticized because of his political duties. If you compare this scene of study with the busy picture of Boniface VIII on page 15, can you understand why?

The pope had a very important role in the Catholic Church. He shaped its religious teaching and explained matters of faith. He was important in appointing clergymen, particularly bishops and archbishops, and supervised the life of monks and nuns. He was also responsible for correcting anyone who held beliefs of which the Church did not approve. The medieval Church taught that there was only one way of worshipping God, and that those who did not follow Church teaching would burn in hell in the next life. For this reason the Church's attitude to people with differing views was very harsh. Jews and Moslems suffered greatly as a result of this intolerance. Christians too were persecuted when scholars who disagreed

13

THE POPE

This altarpiece shows St Peter holding the keys of heaven which Jesus Christ had given him. Medieval popes claimed that their authority was handed down from St Peter and Christ. Because of this they claimed power over every part of people's lives.

with official teaching were silenced, and heretics (see p. 37–39) were burnt at the stake.

From time to time the pope held great councils at which matters of faith were discussed. The councils were attended by clergymen from the whole of Europe. Sometimes even kings were summoned to attend. One of the most important councils of the Middle Ages was held by Innocent III in 1215.

A political ruler

But these were not the pope's only duties. He was not just a spiritual leader, he was also involved in politics. Not only did the pope actually rule part of Italy, he also claimed that all the kings of Europe should obey him in matters of politics. This was a point on which there was much conflict.

Innocent III's words at the start of this chapter were part of this story of conflict. His letter caused much argument when it was written. But he was not the first pope to lay claim to such sweeping power. Throughout the Middle Ages successive popes outlined the powers and responsibilities they believed they ought to exercise. Today we do not always think of popes and bishops playing a part in politics. In the Middle Ages it was different. To understand why many people accepted that the pope should have a role in government, we need to look at the way religion affected people's thoughts.

In the Middle Ages, religious beliefs influenced almost every aspect of life. Religious faith was very strong. As the head of the Church, the pope was

therefore enormously important. On this, everyone agreed. But some scholars went much further than this. They argued that the pope should tell even kings and princes what to do. This doctrine of papal power brought many conflicts.

The pope challenged

There were many who criticized the position of the pope. Some disagreed with the idea that he should exercise political power. Others believed that the pope was too wealthy and too little concerned with religious matters.

Out of this questioning spirit, the movement towards the Protestant Reformation was born. Many were not content to accept the pope's teaching. They appealed instead to their own conscience, and directly to what was written in the Bible.

One medieval writer said that the Pope ruled over the Church 'like a king in a kingdom'. Pope Boniface VIII is shown here attending to business with some of his most important clergymen.

THE BISHOP

This is how one contemporary saw the medieval world:

'There are in society three orders of people. Those whose work it is to pray, those whose work is to fight and those whose work is to labour.'

The work of prayer

The bishop was one of those whose work it was to pray. A bishop is the priest at the head of a diocese (one of the territorial units into which the Church is divided). During the Middle Ages, bishops were regarded as very important people, second in rank only to archbishops. The bishop was responsible for overseeing every aspect of Church life in his diocese. He had to give advice to the clergy, and check that they were leading good lives. From time to time he visited the whole diocese to see that the church buildings were kept in a good state of repair, and that the people were practising their religion. He was also responsible for confirming young children in their faith, and for training and ordaining priests. The chief church of the diocese was the cathedral. This was the bishop's church. Here he led the people in saying Mass and worshipping God.

Obligations to the king

But medieval bishops had other duties besides the work of prayer. They had obligations to the king. These meant that sometimes the life of prayer had to take second place to political and administrative duties. If we examine the careers of some renowned medieval bishops, you will see this very clearly.

This is what one chronicle had to say about Odo, Bishop of Bayeux, one of the men who helped Duke William of Normandy to conquer England in 1066:

'He was the foremost man after the King. He was master of the land when the King was in Normandy. He built many castles throughout the land.'

Odo was a bishop, yet he also had to help the king govern the country. The king appointed Odo to look after the kingdom during his absence. The duties he pressed on Odo meant that he was even involved in castle-building and warfare.

Odo was not the only bishop who had a role in government. Bishops acted as judges, as ambassadors to foreign countries, as army leaders and as financial advisers. In twelfth-century England, some bishops helped to establish the Exchequer, which controlled the king's finances.

Bishops were asked to perform these tasks because they were some of the most highly educated men of the time. The king needed officials who could read and write, and it was hard to find such men outside the Church. The great men of the Church were thus caught up in the world of politics.

Here you can see a bishop blessing a church. The bishop was responsible for the religious life of the people throughout his diocese.

Conflict and compromise

Bishops frequently found themselves in an awkward position. They served the king, but they also owed obedience to the pope. If king and pope disagreed, which side should they take?

This question was solved in different ways in different countries. Sometimes it had dramatic and violent

These pictures tell the story of Thomas Becket, Archbishop of Canterbury in England. He was murdered by a group of knights (bottom left) in his cathedral. Becket was made a Saint, and pilgrims flocked to worship at his shrine (bottom right).

results. In England in the twelfth century the question ended in bloodshed. The Archbishop of Canterbury, Thomas Becket, and the King, Henry II, took opposing views about where the bishops' loyalty should lie. Becket had once been happy for the Church to work with the king's government. When he became archbishop he changed. '*The clergy have Christ alone as king*,' he said. Henry was furious because Becket's words seemed to deny his power. Legend says he demanded, '*Who will rid me of this turbulent priest?*' Four knights overheard him and, thinking that they would earn Henry's gratitude, murdered Becket.

Becket's story was very dramatic. Seldom did bishops lose their lives like this. But all bishops had to face the sort of questions that Becket faced. They had to decide how much they would become involved in politics and how much support they would give the king.

THE KNIGHT

This thirteenth-century writer tells us something of what it meant to be a knight in the Middle Ages:

'"Listen my nephew," said the King. "Now that you have become a knight, give some thought to the glory of knighthood. Behave like a true knight at all times. Be truthful and modest and generous and loyal. Be courteous to the poor and gentle to women." With this, the King handed him his shield.'

Tournaments like the one shown here were popular occasions. Great tents were set up, and people crowded to watch the knights show off their skill with their weapons.

An ideal figure

The writer of these words was German, but he was expressing general ideas about knighthood, and people all over Europe would have agreed with him.

Compare his view of knighthood with this:

'There was a knight, a very honourable man,
Who from the first day he began to campaign
Loved chivalry, truth, honour, freedom and courtesy.'

Not all knights behaved like this. These writers are describing an ideal, a model for knights to follow. This ideal of knightly behaviour is called chivalry. The Church influenced this ideal. It felt that society was becoming violent and lawless and worried about what would happen if powerful, wealthy, armed men like the knights were not restricted in the way they behaved. The ideal of chivalry developed to provide a standard of civilized behaviour for these warriors. Knights were expected to behave with special chivalry towards women. Many knights dedicated themselves to one particular lady — often someone else's wife. They took part in tournaments and jousting competitions hoping to do well and win the favour of their chosen lady.

Reality: the warrior

The knight was a warrior, the most important soldier in the medieval army. He fought on horseback, came dressed in protective armour, and carried expensive weapons. It was considered a great honour to be a knight. The king himself was one. So too were his vassals.

We have seen that when the king granted fiefs to his vassals, they promised to give him military support when he needed it. It was the service of knights which the king chiefly wanted. He would tell his vassals exactly how many knights he expected them to bring to fight for him. In the early Middle Ages, the vassal often just had to remember the number. Later it was more often written down on a piece of parchment in the form of a charter. The number of knights varied. Some vassals had to find up to 60. Others found only one.

One charter about land and knight service said:

This shield was made in Flanders in the fifteenth century. It shows a knight in armour kneeling before his lady. Can you see his helmet and pole-axe?

'*King Richard of England sends greetings to every man who sees this charter or who hears it read out. I want you to know that I have given land in Levens to my trusty Gilbert Fitz Reinfrid, to hold by the service of one knight, and there are many witnesses to my gift.*'

Charters like this were drawn up all over Europe.

They said who gave the land, who was to have the use of it, where the land was, how many knights the recipient was to find in return, and who had witnessed the grant of land.

Becoming a knight

Originally, any knight could make another soldier a knight. A man was knighted as a reward for bravery on the battlefield. The knight-to-be would kneel and receive a hefty sword blow, and that was that. He was pronounced a knight.

In the later Middle Ages things were very different. An elaborate ritual had grown up. By this time it was customary for the king to confer, or grant, knighthood. Instead of taking place on the battlefield, the ceremony usually took place in church. All through the night before, the candidate for knighthood would stay in church, praying to be made worthy of his new life.

One chronicler describes a typical ceremony, when four Irish kings were knighted by the king of England:

'They were knighted by the hand of King Richard in the cathedral church of Dublin, on a Thursday. All the Wednesday night they kept vigil in the cathedral. At mass next morning they were made knights with great solemnity.'

This particular event took place at the end of the fourteenth century. Prayers were said over the knights' swords, dedicating them to God's service.

THE PILGRIM

In this passage from a medieval story, the writer describes the sort of clothes worn by pilgrims:

'Tristan could see two pilgrims advancing. They wore cloaks of linen, and sea-shells and other tokens from foreign lands were sewn on the outside of their clothes. Each carried a staff in his hand.'

Throughout the Middle Ages, pilgrims flocked to the shrines of saints to pray. Some went on pilgrimage again and again. Some travelled a few miles to worship local saints, others went great distances, to Rome or Jerusalem.

Asking for miracles

A letter written in the fifteenth century by the wife of a knight explains why medieval people went on pilgrimage. She was writing to her husband, who had been ill, and told him that she would go on pilgrimage to pray for his recovery.

'I thank God that you are better after the great disease that you have had, for I have had no rest from the time that we first heard of your sickness. I will go on pilgrimage for you.'

This medieval stained glass comes from Canterbury, England, and shows three pilgrims. Hundreds of pilgrims went to Canterbury to pray at the tomb of St Thomas Becket. Many made offerings of jewels, gold or money.

Medieval people believed that the saints had power to work miracles. In their prayers they asked the saints to help them. It was thought to be a mark of special devotion to go on pilgrimage to the place where a saint was buried, or where his or her relics were kept. (A relic is an object that is believed to have belonged to a saint, or even to have been a part of his or her body.) Prayers at such places were thought to be more powerful than those made somewhere else.

At places of pilgrimage, people would beg for a cure

The decoration in medieval churches was designed to teach the people in the congregation about their religion. This window shows a saint, the cross on which Jesus Christ was crucified, and a woman being cured of madness. Its message was that God worked miracles and healed the sick.

for illness or for their sins to be forgiven. This is what the knight's wife meant to do. Other pilgrims went to give thanks, perhaps because they had already been made well. Some went as a penance, that is as a sign that they had committed an act for which they were sorry. There were also those who simply went along for the ride – people who wanted to escape from home for a while, for whom a pilgrimage was a carefree holiday.

Centres of pilgrimage

Christians had made pilgrimages to Jerusalem since the third century. The number of pilgrims grew and grew. By the eleventh century, pilgrimage was international. The greatest centres were Jerusalem, Rome and Compostella in Spain.

But every country had its own saints, and those people who could not make a pilgrimage overseas went to worship at a shrine nearer home. The tomb of St Thomas Becket in Canterbury Cathedral and the shrine of St Cuthbert in Durham were the most popular destinations for English pilgrims. In France, people visited St Denis, Vézelay and Rocamadour.

Pilgrims to Jerusalem wanted to see for themselves the places described in the Bible. It was the ultimate goal for any Christian. To journey to Jerusalem, however, the pilgrim had to endure hardship and fear.

First there was the sea journey, with the threat of pirates, storms, and shipwreck – or simply being swindled by the boatmen. On arrival, relations with the Saracens, as the Moslem inhabitants of the country were called, were sometimes strained. Pilgrims needed safe conducts to protect them as they travelled.

Setting out on pilgrimage

The most famous description of what it was like to set out on pilgrimage was written by the medieval poet, Chaucer. His great work, the *Canterbury Tales*, tells us about a group of pilgrims who leave London to travel to the tomb of St Thomas Becket. Along the way, they tell stories and jokes to amuse themselves, and one of them plays the bagpipes.

It was the custom to bring a souvenir back from pilgrimage. Each centre had its own badge. Jerusalem had a palm leaf. Because of this, pilgrims who went there were called palmers. Compostella had a cockle shell. In Rome, pilgrims bought a badge showing the cloth, or 'vernicle', of St Veronica.

Later in the Middle Ages, the cult of relics began to cause bitter controversy, or argument. Some people questioned whether they were genuine. Venice boasted a tooth belonging to Goliath, the giant killed by David in the Old Testament. Pilgrims to one church in Rome were told that, because they had visited the place, they would never be struck by lightning. Sceptics challenged these ideas. They said that many relics were forgeries. Little by little, belief in the power of saints and relics became less strong. After the Protestant Reformation in the Church in the sixteenth century, fewer people went on pilgrimage.

Many people wore a special costume to show that they were going on pilgrimage. They wore a rough woollen robe, a round felt hat, and carried a long wooden staff. At their destination they might buy a pilgrim badge like this to sew on their clothes.

THE LADY

St Augustine, one of the most famous philosophers of the Christian Church, wrote that:

'The husband should give orders to the wife, parents to the children, and masters should give orders to servants.'

Rights of women

When you read this passage, you will see that women were not considered equal to men in the Middle Ages. St Augustine put them in the same category as children and servants. They had no power to take important decisions for themselves. Until a woman married, she had to obey her father. After that, she was in her husband's power. If she did not do as she was told, she could be severely beaten.

Marriage

Women of the upper classes were married off by their parents. They rarely had any choice. A husband was chosen from a suitable background. Marriage forged links between important families. It was looked upon as a way to increase the wealth or prestige of each family, not as a love match between two individuals.

Nuns in an abbey church. Unmarried women were a burden to their families. Many were sent to become nuns.

When a marriage took place, the bride's father had to provide gifts for the girl to take to her new family. These formed her 'dowry'. Giving a dowry meant that it was expensive to have too many daughters.

For the husband's family, this meant that marriage was a good way of obtaining land and wealth. Rich heiresses would always have many suitors.

Because marriage was so important, girls were married at an early age, sometimes before they were ten. The husband might be much older, perhaps in his

The law gave women very little power, but the wives of important men had to be able to run their lands when their husbands were away at war. Here you can see a great lady out riding with her advisers. They are inspecting the estate.

forties or fifties. When he died, his widow would still be quite young. Her lord or her family would probably pressurize her to marry again. This could happen three or four times in the course of her life. The Church did not allow divorce.

The lady's duties

By reading what people at the time wrote, we can find out what life was like for these women. Although the law gave her very little power, a wife was expected to carry out a great many duties to ensure her husband's household ran smoothly. A French writer describes some of her household tasks:

'She must know how much money comes from the estates, and arrange to live without debts. She must know about the law. She must check the accounts which the servants bring to her. She must know which crops should be planted on the estates, and which fields are best. She will make sure her workers are not lazy, and that the shepherds tend the sheep well. With her women, she will spin and weave clothing for the whole household.'

Upper class women all over Europe had duties like these.

Entering a convent

A rich man's unmarried daughters were often sent to become nuns. An unmarried woman had no position in society. She was a burden to her family. By sending her to a convent, her family solved their problem. What did it mean for the woman, and for the convent? To help you decide, listen to some contemporaries.

This is the voice of a famous French woman called Heloise. She lived in the twelfth century, and became a nun after falling in love with a man of whom her family disapproved.

'It was not because I felt God calling me that I came to accept the severe way of life of the cloister as a young girl. It was because of your desire alone.'

Now see what the fourteenth-century poet, Chaucer, had to say. He describes a prioress, the nun at the head of a priory. The things which worried her most, according to Chaucer, were table manners, clothes, jewellery and her pet dogs.

It seems as if the custom of sending unmarried daughters to convents meant that some nuns were very unhappy. Chaucer's prioress longed for the way of life she had left, and tried to recreate it at the convent. But the results were not always bad. Heloise had entered the convent reluctantly, but she became renowned for her learning, and rose to become an abbess.

This hunting scene comes from a tapestry made in Flanders in the fifteenth century. Historians examine things made in the past to find out about the way people used to live. What does the tapestry tell us about women's costume, and the sports they enjoyed?

THE HERALD

Here the poet Chaucer describes how heralds identified bodies on the battlefield:

*'By coat of arms and crest upon the head
The heralds knew, for all the filth and mud,
That they were Princes of the royal blood.'*

Distinguishing signs

When a knight went into battle, he wore protective armour from head to foot. In a helmet and visor, his face could not be seen. How could he distinguish the enemy from the men on his own side? How could they tell who he was?

The next passage will give you a clue. It was written in the fourteenth century, and describes an army on campaign. The king, his barons, and knights, set out on their horses:

*'Many a fine pennon was fixed on the lance
And many a banner was displayed.'*

What was on these flags? They bore designs which identified the men who carried them. Not only were the designs carried on the flags, they were also painted on shields, and each horse wore a coat with its owner's designs on it. Sometimes the knights themselves wore short tunics bearing the designs over their armour. Because of this, the design became known as a coat of arms.

What sort of designs were used? Some were pictorial — such as a lion, a shell, a dragon, a feather, or a fish. Others were geometric — like a cross, or a zigzag design.

The work of the herald

Someone had to keep a note of all the designs in use, and who they belonged to. This was the herald's job. He wrote details of the coats of arms on long strips of parchment. Sometimes they were so long that the easiest way to store them was to wind them round and round in a roll. The historians who use them today call them heraldic rolls.

To save having to draw coats of arms each time, a special way of describing them in words developed. Heralds always described the coat of arms painted on a shield as though they were standing behind the shield, and carrying it themselves. So if they said the design was on the left side of the shield, everyone would know they meant the left hand of the man who carried it, not the left hand of someone standing in front, looking at it.

When describing a coat of arms, the herald gave the colour of the background first of all. This was called the 'field'. The colours were given in a standard way. 'Or' meant yellow, 'argent' meant white, 'gules' was red, 'azure' blue and 'sable' black. Then they described the 'charge', which was any design placed on the 'field' (background). All the other details were described in a fixed order. A description of a coat of arms in this heraldic language is called a 'blazon'.

Each knight wanted his own coat of arms. With a limited number of colours and shapes to use, this became more difficult. It needed an expert eye to tell the various coats of arms apart. The differences between them were minute.

Disputes sometimes flared up when two different people claimed the right to the same coat of arms. Heralds would be called in to judge such questions.

Look at the shield carried by the knight defending the tower. The coat of arms on the shield enables us to identify him. His name was Sir Andrew de Harcla. He lived in the city of Carlisle in the fourteenth century.

Messengers and commentators

Kings and noblemen employed heralds to act as messengers and commentators. They also used them as ambassadors on diplomatic missions. At tournaments,

Over his armour, the knight wore a coat of arms with his own distinctive design. He could then be identified in battle.

the great fights arranged to show off knightly skills, heralds acted as commentators and announcers, telling the crowded audience which men were fighting. In 1344 King Edward III of England decided to found a society for the bravest knights of the day. They were to be known as the knights of the Blue Garter. The King gave a great feast to celebrate. Heralds were sent to many royal courts to announce his plan. The chronicler Froissart describes the preparations:

'The king sent his heralds to announce it in France, Scotland, Burgundy, Hainault, Flanders, Brabant and also in the German Empire.'

THE MONK

This is a medieval account of how one monastery was founded:

'The king's son gave some land to found a monastery. He planned to visit the monastery often in the future, to pray and hear the word of God. He firmly believed that the daily prayers of the monks would be of great help to him.'

The monks' way of life

These words tell us what people at the time considered to be the most important aspect of the monks' way of life – prayer. Devoting themselves solely to God, monks or nuns shut themselves away from society and spent their time in prayer and meditation.

Monastic life was highly organized. The daily timetable used in many monasteries or convents dated back to the late fifth century. It was drawn up by St Benedict in Italy. This 'Rule' of life was soon used by monks all over Europe. The monks who followed it became known as members of the Benedictine Order. There was also a similar Order created for women, of Benedictine nuns, started by St Benedict's sister, St Scholastica.

Monks and nuns spent their time in worship. This medieval glass shows two monks at prayer.

The Benedictine Rule gave a pattern to each day. First place was given to the round of prayer. This was the *Opus Dei* (Latin for the 'work of God'). Then there was manual work in the fields to produce food for the monastery. There was also work in part of the monastery called the 'cloister'. This was a covered walk around four sides of a square at the heart of the monastery. Here the monks studied, or wrote out prayers and parts of the Bible. At this time, the only way to produce books was to copy them by hand. The monks wrote very carefully, decorating their work with gold leaf and coloured pictures like the ones in this book. Nuns would not study but would spend time in tasks like sewing clothes for the poor, or preparing medicines.

When people became monks or nuns, they made three vows. They swore to give up all their personal possessions. This was the vow of poverty. They promised to remain single – the vow of chastity. Finally, they promised to obey the head of the monastery or abbey, the abbot or abbess. That was the vow of obedience.

Many people became monks and nuns because the monastic way of life was highly thought of. This picture shows a man receiving the tonsure – having his head shaved on top – and dedicating himself to God.

New orders

As time went by, the Benedictines lost popularity. They were criticized for a number of reasons. Some monasteries had become wealthy. Some monks failed to keep their vows. New Orders of monks were founded by enthusiasts who wanted to change these things.

One new order was the Cistercian Order. The Order became respected at once. Those lacking the ability to learn all the Latin prayers for the services could still have a place with the Cistercians. They became lay-brothers, or *conversi*. Lay-brothers helped work on the monastery estates and joined in what services they could in church. Over 700 Cistercian houses were founded in Europe.

Monks, nuns and the outside world

The monastic way of life was highly thought of. Many people chose to become monks or nuns. But not everyone felt they could endure the discipline of monastic life. People who wanted to show how much they respected this way of life, but who did not want to take religious vows themselves, gave gifts to the monasteries or convents. Some, like the king's son in the story at the beginning of the chapter, gave enough land to build a new religious house. In return for their gifts, they asked the monks and nuns to pray for them.

Such gifts brought problems for the monks and nuns. They were difficult to refuse, and in time there were monasteries that became wealthy as a result. Some monks found that they were not as cut off from society as they had intended. They had extensive estates to run and workers to supervise.

For these reasons criticism of monks and nuns grew. It was not long before the Cistercians and other new Orders were criticized as much as the Benedictines. The fourteenth-century English poet, Langland, attacked those monks whose only interests were eating, drinking and acquiring more land. Throughout Europe many people felt as he did. This spirit of dissatisfaction helped to lead eventually to the reforms in the Church in the sixteenth century known as the Protestant Reformation.

Not all monks and nuns managed to live up to their vows. Like ordinary people, some committed crimes and were punished. Here a monk is sitting in the stocks.

THE DOCTOR

Giving advice to his contemporaries, a medieval surgeon wrote that:

'To close the edges of a wound, you must make ants bite on them, and then cut off their heads.'

Reading these words, you might assume that medieval medicine was superstitious and backward. Certainly many strange beliefs influenced the way

This picture shows men gathering plants for use as medicine. Many medieval remedies were made from plants.

medieval people looked at disease. But there were reasons for all these beliefs.

Scientific knowledge

In Ancient Greece, medicine had reached sophisticated levels. But most Greek scientific texts had been forgotten in Christian Europe. They had survived in the Arab world, and from the twelfth century onwards they were gradually translated into Latin, the language of European scholarship.

There were many scientific theories taken for granted today which were unknown in the Middle Ages. The connection between bad hygiene and disease had not been made. No one knew how blood circulated round the body, nor the precise functions of the organs of the body. There were no injections. The equipment used was less technologically advanced than today's — there were no microscopes, for example.

Disease and death

Because of these things, the causes of illness were less properly understood. When in 1347–49, a plague called the Black Death swept through Europe, people believed a strange gas in the air must be responsible. They were powerless to do anything about it. Almost a third of the population died.

This is how one chronicler describes the panic at the time:

'Corpses were abandoned in empty houses. No one would bury them for fear of the disease, and none would go near those who were ill.'

Even in normal years, however, life expectancy was very low. A man who lived for forty-five years would be thought to have reached a ripe old age. The wealthy usually lived longer than the poor. They had a better diet and a more comfortable life.

Contemporary pictures tell us about the illnesses people had and the way they were treated. Blood-letting was often prescribed as a cure. Here you can see how it was carried out.

A visit from the doctor

The doctors of the rich and poor were different too. In the countryside, people relied on herbal treatments. They took herbs like yarrow, hellebore, rue, lupin roots, mustard, ivy, or laurel leaves, and drank them in water, or turned them into ointments. Often one of the local women would advise which herbs were best. She was known as a wise woman. Modern medicine substitutes chemicals for herbs, but often the treatment is similar.

The wealthy could afford more expensive treatment. They could call in a trained doctor. An Italian living in the twelfth century describes a typical doctor's visit:

'A doctor should put the patient at ease before he starts the examination. Then the doctor takes the pulse for at least one hundred beats.'

This sounds like modern medicine. The prescriptions and treatments do not. Because it was believed that many illnesses were caused by 'bad' blood (or by too much blood) a treatment that was widely used was 'blood-letting' — opening a vein or artery and letting the patient bleed for a while. It was thought that this had to be done at certain phases of the moon to work well.

Medicines were concocted out of strange ingredients, from dung-beetles, to bat droppings, to powdered earthworm. They were prepared by a person called an apothecary. When King Edward I of England was dying, his doctors prescribed herbal baths, pomegranate wine, and a syrup made of precious stones like pearls. Gold was one of the most highly esteemed ingredients.

In comparison with today, doctors had a fairly limited range of treatments. Contemporary drawings show us some of the things they did. They set broken bones, dressed wounds, lanced abscesses, and treated some infections. Surgery was dangerous. There was no completely safe or scientific way to put the patient to sleep. Surgeons had their methods. Powerful drugs like hemlock were used. But there were no painkillers, and no antiseptics when — if — the patient came round.

This picture shows an eye operation in progress. At this time there were many diseases which could not be successfully treated. Some people died from illnesses which could be cured today.

THE HERETIC

This is the voice of a fourteenth-century heretic who belonged to a sect called the Cathars:

'The priests cannot save souls. Only the goodmen of our faith can do this.'

The writer considered himself a good Christian, but he no longer believed all the teachings of the Church.

Obedience to the Church

Religion affected almost every aspect of the way people lived in the Middle Ages. The Church taught that there was only one true religion, Christianity, and only one way to follow it – through the Catholic Church.

'*Obedience is the greatest good*,' said one fourteenth-century pope. The laity (all those who were not clergy) were expected to obey the Church absolutely in matters of faith. In this climate of thought, how do you think the Church reacted to people who started to think for themselves about religion? What would happen if they questioned Church teaching, and disagreed with it?

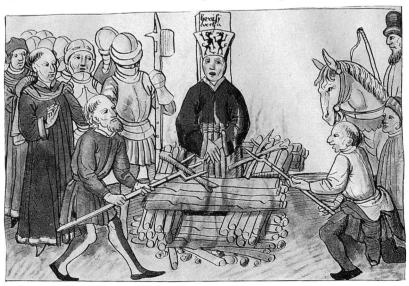

In Bohemia (modern Czechoslovakia), Jean Huss was burnt at the stake for heresy because he questioned the Pope's position in the Church.

The Church did not tolerate different opinions in matters of religion. Here Pope Urban II is shown preaching a famous sermon which urged Christians to embark on the first crusade, or holy war, against the Saracens.

Choosing what to believe

People who did this were called heretics. It is a word which comes from the Greek language, and means 'someone who wants to choose for themselves'. When the Church used the word, it meant someone who preferred to choose what to believe for themselves, rather than accept Church teaching.

In the eleventh and twelfth centuries, the Church became alarmed at the increasing number of heretics. Until this time, very few people had rejected its teaching. Now suddenly all sorts of heretical beliefs were being put forward. The Church felt its authority was being threatened.

Different beliefs

One of the most dominant heresies was Catharism. It was particularly strong in the south of France. Cathars believed that the world was evil, and so was the Church along with it. To obtain everlasting life, believers had only to take part in one special religious rite (ceremony), just before they died. This rite was organized by the Cathars themselves. The Cathars pursued their ideas to extremes. Believing the world was evil, they prohibited marriage, because marriage would lead to children, and so the world would continue. They would not eat meat, or eggs, or other animal products, because this meant that the animal kingdom would go on reproducing itself.

Not all heresies were quite as extraordinary as Catharism. Some seemed to accept part of the Church's teaching, but wanted to make changes and reform it. A number of heresies were very close to traditional belief. It was just the crucial question of obedience to the authority of the Church which set them apart.

Some wanted the laity to play a greater role in religion. They demanded that the Bible should be translated from Latin into their own language, so they could understand it better. This was the aim of Peter Waldo, a merchant who lived in Lyons in France in the eleventh century. His followers were known as the Poor Men of Lyons because, inspired by the Gospels, they gave away all their possessions. Their ideas were popular in the Netherlands and the German Empire.

The Church tried many ways to persuade heretics that their views were wrong. Books which put forward heresy were burned.

The Church responds

The Church condemned Waldo's teaching. Condemnation took many forms. Heretics could be hanged, or even burnt at the stake, if they refused to give up their beliefs.

It is difficult for us to understand how the Church could uphold such methods. But because the Church taught that heretics who did not change their beliefs would go to hell, some people believed it was right to use even torture and execution to force heretics to change.

THE MASON

The chronicler Froissart described the way building work was organized in the Middle Ages:

'In the year 1343 a great building project was begun at Windsor castle. Workmen were brought in from all over England.'

Arranging for a large number of masons to work on the site was the first requirement.

The work of the mason

Only the most important buildings were made of stone in the Middle Ages. Work on great stone churches and castles called for a large labour force. Here you see construction work on a tower.

The master mason was one of the most highly skilled workers of the Middle Ages. He combined the roles which architect, engineer, sculptor and builder perform today. He worked on all the stages of a building project, from the plans and design to the construction itself. Many men worked under him.

Most masons were 'itinerant' craftsmen. That meant they travelled from one site to another, rather than always living and working in one place. A few great cathedrals had a permanent workforce, so that masons were on hand to carry out new work or repairs at any time. But usually masons had to move on when their job was done.

While they were employed, masons lived at the place where they were working. They would set up a number of work shops, called lodges, and here they worked, ate, and sometimes slept. They organized their work very strictly, electing a master mason to govern them. He was responsible for the quality of their work, and also had to supervise the apprentices — young men who were training to become masons.

The buildings

Few buildings were built of stone at this time. Most were made of wood. Great numbers of workmen were needed to build the large stone castles and churches of the time. 'Free' masons performed the finest work. Less qualified masons shaped the blocks of stone and then laid them in place.

When historians look at architecture, they find that many buildings of the same date share common characteristics. The clergymen and nobles who financed great projects followed current fashions in architecture. They wanted to copy new buildings elsewhere. In this way fashions spread all over Europe. The Normans who conquered England in the eleventh century were keen to build churches in the style with which they were familiar. This is why many similarities exist between great English churches of this period and Norman ones.

But buildings could not have been copied like this without the itinerant masons. Throughout the Middle Ages, masons moving from one area to another took with them particular ideas about decoration and methods of working, so that the same style might spread over much of Europe.

This detailed figure sculpture comes from Laon Cathedral in France. The master mason often combined the role of architect, sculptor and building supervisor.

Tools and equipment

To begin with, the master mason drew up a plan for the building. Foundations were dug, and then the building could start. Once the walls became too high to work on, scaffolding was put up. It was made from poles tied together, and was erected in stages. Once the wall again rose out of reach, the scaffolding was taken down, and put up again on top of the wall. To hoist heavy blocks of stone into position on top of the walls, a pulley and windlass were used. There were no power tools — just hand tools, like axes, hammers and cold chisels to cut the stone.

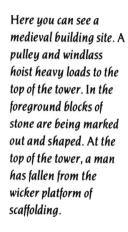

Here you can see a medieval building site. A pulley and windlass hoist heavy loads to the top of the tower. In the foreground blocks of stone are being marked out and shaped. At the top of the tower, a man has fallen from the wicker platform of scaffolding.

The site was a dangerous place to work. It was not unusual for men to be killed in falls from scaffolding. There was always the possibility that a part of the new building might come crashing down. Trying to build across the roof space of great churches was always a problem. First a temporary wooden framework was put up, resting on top of the columns in the nave (the main part of the church). Ribs of stone were placed on top of the wooden frame, and cemented together. More stone was then used to fill in the space between the ribs. The next stage was to remove the wooden framework in the centre. Timing was critical. If the mortar had not yet set, disaster struck. This happened at Beauvais Cathedral in France, in 1284, when a vault collapsed completely.

THE MERCHANT

T hese few lines are a key to understanding the work of medieval merchants:

'For lack of money I forego many good bargains,' grumbled a fifteenth-century merchant. *'Let me know what ready money I have at Bruges.'*

Trade and travel

Trade — buying and selling at a profit — was the chief preoccupation of the merchant. You can see that very clearly in the words above. When you also know that the quotation comes from a letter written in London, and sent to a business colleague in Europe, you can see another important fact about the merchant's life. Trade meant travel. It might be local travel, over a fairly small area, or it might involve a great journey across many countries. One thing was certain: the merchant was frequently on the move.

It was rare for a village or town to be self-sufficient, that is to be capable of making all the food, clothing and material goods it needed. The poorer a village, or even a household, was, the more it would have to try to live just on what it could produce itself. But if there was a little left over once everyone's basic needs were satisfied, this could be sold. Then there was money available to buy something a little more luxurious — like pepper or some spices to liven up a monotonous meal . . . ribbons or cloth to make brighter clothes . . .

In much of Europe in the twelfth century, this is what happened. Methods of agriculture were being improved, and more food was produced. This 'surplus' (extra) made it possible for some people to devote their time to trade and industry, rather than having to farm the land. Commerce flourished.

Medieval glass provides us with evidence about people's life and work. This window comes from Tournai in the Low Countries, and shows merchants' goods being weighed. Glass was rare and expensive. With their profits, merchants could afford to have windows like this set up in church.

Luxuries from the East and the Mediterranean were especially desired. Spices, fruits like oranges and lemons, silks, dyes for cloth, sweet wines, Italy's fine clothes and jewellery — these were mainly rich men's purchases. So too was German metalwork in silver and gold, German armour, French wine, Flemish cloth from Belgium. The Scandinavian countries (Norway, Sweden, Finland, Denmark) exported furs, timber and fish; Spain traded its leather, and England its wool. There was even a brisk trade in slaves, most of whom came from eastern Europe.

The Bishop of Paris, France, blessing a fair. Merchants travelled to fairs like this all over Europe. Look at the stalls set up to display their goods.

Fairs

Buyers and sellers met at the great fairs which were held each year. They often lasted several weeks. Here merchants from all over Europe would gather. So too would hordes of other people. Wealthy lords and ladies would send servants to buy a year's stock of spices, sugar, or cloth. Great monasteries would send their officials on similar errands.

And for the local village people, it was a holiday, a time to go and enjoy the hustle-bustle atmosphere and gaze at the amazing things they might never have seen before, and would certainly never be able to afford. The word fair comes from the Latin word *feriae*, which means holiday.

Each country held fairs of its own. One of the most important in England was held at Stourbridge in the Midlands. It lasted for three weeks each September. It was laid out like a small town — a maze of alleyways, crammed with booths.

Here you could buy horses, soap, honey, coal, salt from Worcester, iron from Sussex. The Dutch brought cheeses to sell, the Greeks almonds and spices. Merchants from Venice sold gems and velvet.

Some cities were completely dominated by the merchants who lived there. North Italy, Flanders (Belgium), and Germany were heavily influenced by their merchant population. The cities of Italy often quarrelled violently and even went to war with each other.

A new way to riches

Trade offered a different way of life from the one most people knew. It began to change people's outlook. A French writer records the general feeling about merchants in the fifteenth century:

'They are very rich. Their wives dress expensively, adopting the style of princesses. But they ought to keep to their own station in life.'

Many people shared her view. They felt that the merchants were arrogant newcomers, who wanted to have the same influence as knights and barons.

Ownership of land was still the most important source of wealth. But now wealth could also be created from trade — and sometimes by men of lower social standing. This was bound to lead to change.

Here you can see grain being unloaded. How is the grain carried? Do the men have any equipment or machinery to help?

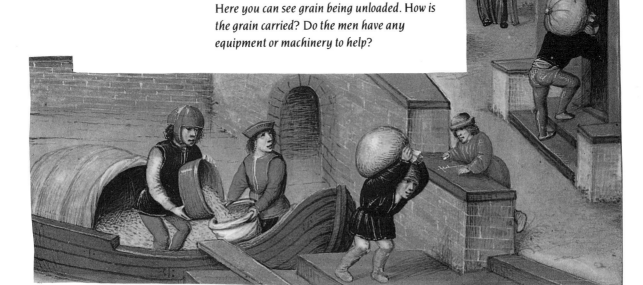

GLOSSARY

Abbess The nun in charge of a religious house in which nuns lived.

Abbot The monk in charge of a religious house in which monks lived.

Apothecary The person who mixed and sold drugs and medicine.

Baron An important nobleman.

Black Death The name given to a mystery disease which swept through Europe in the years 1347–9, killing thousands of people. Modern scientists have identified it as bubonic plague.

Blood-letting A common medical treatment in the Middle Ages. A vein was cut open, and the patient allowed to bleed for a short time.

Charter A document written on a piece of parchment. Charters were used to make announcements or grant important rights.

Chivalry The code of behaviour for knights. They were encouraged to be brave and loyal, and to defend the poor and weak.

Chronicle A record of events.

Coat of arms A distinctive heraldic design which identified the knight who wore it.

Conversi Lay-brothers in a monastery. Lay-brothers did not take part in all the religious services, but spent much time helping the monks by doing manual work.

Doctrine The teaching of the Church on matters of religion.

Domesday Book A survey of nearly all the lands in England, carried out by the officials of King William I, and completed in 1086.

Dowry The gifts which a bride's family had to provide for her husband and his family when a marriage took place.

Estate The lands of a wealthy person.

Feudal system A word historians use to describe medieval society. In theory, every man had a lord whom he obeyed, receiving land and protection in return. For example, the peasant served the lord of the manor, and the lord of the manor served the king. In reality it was very much more complicated.

Fief An estate granted by one person to another. The person who received the fief would swear to serve the other loyally in return.

Herald The person who kept records to identify knights by looking at their coats of arms. Many heralds were also employed as messengers and diplomats.

Heretic Someone who disagreed with the teaching of the Church, and was condemned by the Church authorities.

Jousting A competition between two knights on horseback. Each rode armed with a lance, trying to knock the other from his horse.

Knight A warrior who fought on horseback. Knights were encouraged to be brave and loyal, and to defend the poor and weak.

Laity All members of the Church who are not clergymen: the congregation.

Lance A weapon used by knights. It was a long wooden shaft with which the knight tried to topple his enemy from his horse.

Magna Carta Latin for *Great Charter*. This was a charter of important liberties granted by King John of England to his barons in 1215.

Pennon A small flag.

Pilgrim Someone who travels to pray at the shrine of a saint.

Protestant Reformation A religious movement which broke away from the Catholic Church in the sixteenth century.

Relics Objects associated with men and women believed to be saints, such as hair, parts of the body and scraps of their clothing. These were treated with great respect. Pilgrims travelled great distances to pray in churches where relics were kept.

Vassal Someone who vowed loyal service and obedience to a lord.

Windlass A mechanism used for lifting heavy objects, by playing out a chain attached to a roller.

FURTHER READING

For Children

Simon Adams, *Trade and Religion – A Historical Atlas*, Kingfisher, 1989.

Mike Corbishley, *The Middle Ages – A Cultural Atlas for Young People*, Facts On File, 1989.

Fiona Macdonald, *The Middle Ages*, Simon & Schuster Young Books, 1991.

W C Sellar and R J Yeatman, *1066 And All That*, Methuen, 1930.

R J Unstead, *Monasteries*, A & C Black, 1970.

For Adults

Emmanuel Le Roy Ladurie, *Montaillou*, Penguin, 1980.

R W Southern, *The Making of the Middle Ages*, Hutchinson, 1967.

R W Southern, *Western Society and the Church in the Middle Ages*, Penguin, 1970.

D M Stenton, *The English Woman in History*, London, 1957.